Praise for 'Creation Under Const

"I spent years trying to hide the 'structural damage' of my life behind quick fixes and a smile. Reading Vivian's work felt like finally being given permission to take off the mask and put on a hard hat. This book met me right in the middle of my own demolition."
 — Jordan S., 34, *Chicago, IL*

"As a creative, I've always struggled with feeling 'unfinished.' These poems spoke to the parts of me that are still under renovation. Vivian has a way of making the grit of faith feel like a beautiful, necessary process rather than something to be ashamed of."
 — Elena R., 28, *Orlando, FL*

"I've read a lot of devotionals, but nothing has ever felt this raw. The Algorithm and Unashamed hit me specifically—they gave language to the internal battles I couldn't explain. It's a relief to know God isn't finished with me yet."
 — Marcus T., 42, *Dallas, TX*

"Creation Under Construction is the spiritual toolbelt I didn't know I needed. The Selah moments forced me to stop running and actually inspect my own foundation. It's honest, it's messy, and it's full of a hope that actually feels real."
 — Sarah L., 31, *Seattle, WA*

"Vivian's spoken-word rhythm jumps off the page. I felt like I was sitting in the room with her, watching the Kintsugi gold fill in my own cracks. This isn't just a book; it's a living testimony for anyone who feels like a work in progress."
 — David P., 55, *Atlanta, GA*

CREATION UNDER CONSTRUCTION

Vivian Figueroa

Dedication

To the Master Architect,
who drew the blueprints long before I knew who I was.

And to my family—my scaffolding and my shelter.
Thank you for loving the work in progress and
helping me become the person I am today.

Welcome to the renovation.

Not the kind that requires permits or power tools, but the kind that requires courage—the willingness to let God into the unfinished spaces of your soul.

Within these pages, you'll find spoken word poems that echo in the chambers of your heart, prayers that speak what you haven't found words for, and reflections that meet you in the rubble and the renewal. This is a devotional for those who know that faith isn't about perfection—it's about transformation. It's about standing in the midst of your own reconstruction and trusting the Master Builder who sees what you're becoming, not just what you've been.

Each day invites you to pick up your tools: questions that excavate truth, prayers that lay new foundations, and moments of stillness where you can hear the sound of hammering—God at work in you, through you, making all things new.

The construction site of your soul is sacred ground. There's dust in the air and work to be done, but there's also promise in every beam raised, every wall restored, every room reimagined.

Let's build something beautiful together.

TABLE OF CONTENTS

Introduction

Before You Enter the Construction Site
I used to think that being a Christian meant being a finished product.
Polished. Perfect. Putting on a show.
I thought if I had cracks in my foundation, the whole building would be condemned. So I hid the mess behind drywall and cheap paint, hoping nobody would notice the structural damage.

But God doesn't condemn the construction site just because it's messy.
He just puts on a hard hat and gets to work.
This book is not a museum of perfect saints. It is a blueprint of a work in progress. It is for the ones who feel like a demolition site.
For the ones who have been told they are a "Mistake."
For the ones whose default setting is shame.

This isn't just a book of poetry to read, it's a tool belt to use.
In these pages, you won't just find rhymes, you will find a place to wrestle.
You will find prayers when you have no words.
You will find space to write when your soul needs to speak.

So, put down the mask.
Take a deep breath.

Welcome to the renovation.
You are not broken beyond repair; you are just **Creation Under Construction.**

12

Introduction

Before you turn the page, I need you to do something: put on your hard hat.

Because a renovation can be overwhelming, I've provided a Project Manual to help you navigate the flow of this journey.

As you walk through these three phases—**The Default, The Construction**, and **The Commission**—you will encounter several recurring elements designed to help you rebuild:

The Anchor– Every section begins here. This is a core truth or a piece of Scripture intended to steady your feet. Before you look at the mess, look at the Anchor. It is the solid ground that holds the weight of everything that follows.

The Poem– These are the stories and the spoken-word rhythms of the work. They are raw, honest, and unvarnished. They describe the demolition of the old self and the spiritual reversion required to let God take the lead.

The Callout– You will come across unique visual pages that highlight a single, high-impact line from the poetry. They are meant to stop you in your tracks and force you to look at a specific revelation until it sinks in.

The Prayer– We end each movement by talking to The Architect. These prayers transition the art into a personal petition. I invite you to make these words your own as you consult with God about the renovation of your soul.

Selah– In ancient songs, Selah was a call to pause and let the music breathe. In this book, these are your Journal Reflections. This is the space for you to pick up the pen. Don't rush past them. Use these moments to inspect your own "fault lines" and write down what God is revealing to you.

You are not broken beyond repair. You are simply a work perpetually under construction. The mess is just proof that He hasn't stopped working on you yet.

Let's get to work.

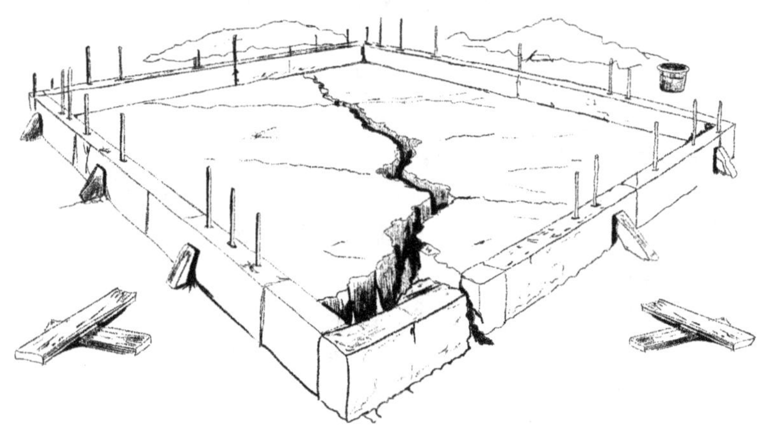

We build our houses on sand
and wonder why the floor is shaking.
It isn't an earthquake, beloved,
it's just the foundation breaking.

PART I:
THE DEFAULT
(The Struggle)

Day 1
CURRENT NEWS

THE ANCHOR

"For God so loved the world that he gave his one and only Son, that whoever believes in him shall not perish but have eternal life. For God did not send his Son into the world to condemn the world, but to save the world through him." — John 3:16–17

THE POEM

Current News
We live in a time where
speech is broken glass
scattering shards of sharp cynicism
you have to tiptoe over,
or else someone picks up
Your words and cuts you with them.

I think it's a trend that stems
From the idea that mainstream beliefs
are the only ones we should hem
into our realities.

We also live in a time where anxieties

affect 3 million cases a year,
3 million chests pounding in fear
The panic begins to set
As our face drowns in tears.
So to fix our inclining stress
We look to Mary Jane's weeds.
The same weed we use to inhale a
Synthetic sense of temporal peace and
Exhale out clouds of poison and
Distorted mentalities.

I've been seeing my generation weeping.
Kids with guns sweeping down schools
Leaving 8 year olds bleeding on the floor
Because of the way other kids have been mistreating.
They're weeping because identity has been lost
And they think God has been sleeping.

God hasn't been sleeping,
He's been pleading and repeating that we need to repent because
Heaven is reeking of the pile high sin that we've been reaping.
The demons are laying back satisfied,
It's what all along they've been dreaming.
Humans have been feeding
on hatred
and deceiving themselves that Christianity
is obsolete.

But it's so much more, it supersedes.
It's a foundation that's sturdier
Than the sand the world builds
it's houses on, it's concrete.
It's John 3:16 complete.
Because God so loved this world

Creation Under Construction

He sent His Son to die on a tree
Just to return to life on day three,
And not only that, but against death himself
would He succeed, steal the keys
and split the veil in two so that Christ could live in
me..... and you.

So current news.
If you haven't guessed already
Jesus is coming soon.
The comforter, The counselor is breaking the story
that yours is still not through.
Current News.

We can change the times that we're living in
By being a light in the darkness, spreading hope and truth.
Instead of words being broken glass,
They will become words that won't fall to the ground like in
2 Samuel 2.
Current News.
I choose to believe,

Will you?

Speech
is broken
glass
you
have to
tiptoe over

THE PRAYER
Father,
I am tired of walking on broken glass. I confess that I have let the anxiety of the world drown out the peace of Your presence. I see the pain in my generation—the weeping, the confusion, the violence—and sometimes I feel helpless.

Thank You that You have not been sleeping. Thank You that You did not leave us to navigate this mess alone. Help me to stop building my life on the shifting sand of cultural trends and plant my feet on the concrete of the Gospel. Make me a light in the darkness. Let my words be healing, not sharp.

In Jesus' Name,
Amen.

SELAH
The poem mentions "mainstream beliefs" that we hem into our realities. What is one belief or fear from the news/culture that you have allowed to influence your peace this week?

____

____

____

____

____

____

____

____

____

____

____

____

Day 2

THE ALGORITHM

THE ANCHOR
"Am I now trying to win the approval of human beings, or of God? Or am I trying to please people? If I were still trying to please people, I would not be a servant of Christ." — Galatians 1:10

THE POEM

The Algorithm
It's 2 AM and the blue light is the only halo I see.
I'm scrolling, patrolling,
Comparing my "behind the scenes" to everyone else's
Highlight reel.
It's a steal,
The way comparison comes in like a thief in the night
To snatch away my joy and leave me with
A blight of insecurity.

I look at the screen and see
Perfection, curated, filtered, and cropped.
While I'm sitting here feeling like my life has flopped.
I'm double-tapping on images that make me feel
Like a single-digit mistake.

<h1 style="text-align:center">The Algorithm</h1>

Asking myself, "How much more of this can I take?"

We trade our identity for an algorithm,
Dancing to the beat of a digital rhythm
That says, "If they don't like it, you don't matter."
But then I hear the shatter.
Not of the glass screen, but of the lie.

Because the God of the universe didn't
Create me for the "For You" page,
He created me for the stage of History!
He doesn't need a filter to see my beauty,
He doesn't need a caption to explain my duty.

I am fearfully and wonderfully made,
Not fearfully and wonderfully displayed.
So I'm putting the phone down.
I'm trading the scroll for the Scroll of Life.
Because likes fade, comments delete, and trends die,
But the love of Jesus is the only verified check
I'll ever need to get by.

THE PRAYER
Lord,
Forgive me for seeking validation from a screen instead of from Your Spirit. I admit that I have let the "likes" of others determine my worth. I have traded my peace for an algorithm that does not know my name.

Remind me today that I am already chosen. I do not need to filter my life for You to love me. Help me to put down the phone and pick up Your Word. I want to live for an audience of One.

Amen.

YOU
were created for
CONNECTION,
not just for
CLICKS
and
CONSUMPTION.

SELAH

Who are you trying to impress right now? If you knew that God was completely satisfied with you at this moment, what would you stop doing?

Day 3

MISTAKE

THE ANCHOR

"I praise you because I am fearfully and wonderfully made; your works are wonderful, I know that full well."
— Psalm 139:14T

THE POEM

Mistake

Webster's dictionary definition of mistake
Is as follows:
An error in action, opinion, or judgement.
This was my self-appointed definition
That I carried for a long time.
I know it's one that you're carrying right now.

In my head a scenario played out
Where somewhere along the way God had
Messed up.
A fumble of the fingers that had made my
Front teeth too large,
Awkwardness accidently sprinkled in
Instead of flawless grace and charm.

Mistake

But before an angel could drag me into the recycle bin,
There I was whisked away to earth.

Some part of the action in my creation was a mistake.
I considered His opinion as platitudes and
Pity statements meant to make me feel better.
Because who could actually love a mistake?

That all changed when I met Jesus.
It transformed everything
He told me, " I see you"
He saw past my flaws, past my blemishes,
Past all the heartache that I've caused Him.
Three words redefined the person that
I made myself out to be.

The Creator of the universe who established
The boundaries of galaxies,
Who told the sea this is how far you can go.
The very same God who fixed the exact conditions
That this earth needed to sustain life,
To the precise degree of tilt of the axis.
No, this God didn't have a fumble of the fingers.
No mishaps can be told in all His creations.

Did you hear that?
You. Aren't. A. Mistake.
And He didn't start with you.
In His word, He tells us that we are:
Accepted, Redeemed,
Chosen, loved beyond measure,
Forgiven, valuable,
Children of God, Saints,
Free, vessels of the Holy Spirit, Beautiful

Full of purpose and so much more!

There is an enemy that wants
You to keep thinking you're a mistake.
He doesn't want you to know your
True value, that you were worth
Dying on the Cross over.
For Jesus to say these three words,
"It is finished."
His sacrifice was for you.
Salvation bought at His expense, for you.
No beloved, you could never be classified
As a mistake, but the crown of all creation.

THE PRAYER

Creator God,

I confess that I have often looked in the mirror and seen an error. I have allowed the definition of "mistake" to cling to me like a label I cannot wash off. Today, I choose to listen to a different voice.

Thank You that there were no fumbles in my creation. Thank You that You do not make accidents. Help me to silence the lies that say I am too much or not enough. I accept the truth that I am chosen, redeemed, and designed on purpose.

In Jesus' Name,

Amen.

You. Aren't. A. Mistake.

And He didn't start with you.

SELAH

What is one physical or personality trait you have called a "flaw" that God might call a "feature"?

Day 4
DEFAULT

THE ANCHOR

"Therefore, there is now no condemnation for those who are in Christ Jesus, because through Christ Jesus the law of the Spirit who gives life has set you free from the law of sin and death."

— Romans 8:1-2

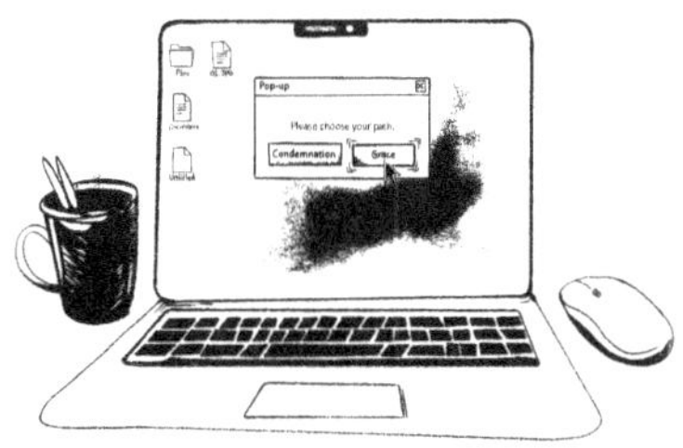

THE POEM

Default

It starts like this.
It seems like no matter how far I get
In knowing more about You,
The moment I fall,
All of that goes right out the window.
You become a God of strict lines
And rigid edges.
Grace doesn't exist,
I'm left to the trenches.
Everything that I know to be true just
Vanishes.
"Would you like to allow condemnation
As your default?"

Creation Under Construction

(Clicks YES)

I sink low in my transgressions
My vices and my concessions.
My thoughts inon repeat, are endless
They're relentless
I can't catch a breath, it's oppressive.
At night these demons
Are aggressive
They come at me like some kind of collective.
Even then I hide,
Searching for the fig leaves
That will cover my indignity.
So just like Adam and Eve,
The moment Your voice calls out in the garden
That's my cue to flee.
"Would you like to allow shame as your default?"

And on and on I continue to add
Lie upon lie.
"I can handle this on my own"
But the burden is heavy,
I'm outdone by my pride.
"The reflection in the mirror is ugly"
What You created, isn't worth a dime.

Let's not even talk about my "calling"
You can't use a dirty, cracked vessel like me
It's useless, no purpose in design.
These lies are ones that i've allowed
Permission to be my defaults.
And so have you.

We fall back to the settings

That satan doesn't want Jesus to undo.
All of these statements that the Cross
Made untrue.
The spilt blood of an innocent man
Who overcame the tomb
Jesus de-faulted you
Not because you had to work at it
There is nothing you can do!
He loves you
He LOVES you
Set your defaults to the truth.
"Would you like to allow Jesus to be your default?"

THE PRAYER

Jesus,

I am so prone to wander back to shame. When I mess up, my instinct is to hide, to find fig leaves, to assume You are angry. Today, I am asking You to reset my spiritual settings.

Thank You that You do not work with strict lines and rigid edges, but with open arms. When the option comes up to choose "Condemnation," give me the strength to click "No." I set my default to Your grace.

Amen.

PRIDEFUL
JEALOUSY
ANGRY
FAULT
INSECURE
DOUBTFUL
Jesus
de-faulted
you.

SELAH

When you sin or make a mistake, what is the very first thought that pops into your head? Is it "I'm sorry" or "I'm worthless"? How can you change that reaction?

Day 5

ENGULFED

THE ANCHOR

"Create in me a clean heart, O God, and renew a right spirit within me."

— Psalm 51:10

THE POEM

Engulfed

Lately when I speak to you
It's as if my words are stuck in a
Slingshot and launched into the air.

Those words were supposed to grow wings and fly
but instead they turned to rocks, dropped, and ended nowhere.
Kinda like the heart that sent them there.

Psalm 51:10 says " Create a clean heart for me and
a right Spirit within me"
So please, God, this is exactly what I need.
The Holy Spirit doing a holy surgery.
Put me under the knife to slice off all the
Weeds.

Engulfed

But not the dandelion kind that blows in the wind when you pick
it up
Instead, thorns that prick and prod at you until you bleed.
And speaking about bleeding,
Lord knows how many holes are in me, cuz
I've been stabbed one too many times by bad company.
With Your expertise, I know you'll stitch me up without a scar to
be seen.
This is why surrender I bring.

I've been swallowed by sin
under the sea of guilt, I'm drowning.
Like Jonah I refused to hear your precious calling.
So instead I tread my own path, thinking
I could find a better option, which was appalling.

Down I sank to the ocean floor,
the seaweed of my blindness
Got me knocking on death's door
until I deplored with you to give
me another chance, Your will for me
I know for certain, has more.

Those three days I sat wallowing,
wondering how is it, I took that detour.
We all think we're stronger and more resilient
in our core.
So we think that it's okay to only tiptoe to the beat
DJ devil drops instead of dance to it.
But here's the secret···
You can't defeat the demons you
enjoy playing with.

Like a matchstick, it's only a matter of time before the fuse of

what you're able to refuse, Burns quick.
When that ends, there enters wickedness.
We become engulfed in the pit that
we ourselves created to hide from God with.

It's all a cycle.
like a boomerang, can't contain all the things that I'm feelin'
all the things that I'm feelin'
Because everytime I do, I'm like a volcano
that's afraid to admit they're about to blow.
A little teapot under pressure,
with lava inside that's pushing to flow
The enemy pulling up a seat cuz he's about to see a show.
I'm being swallowed whole
and given misery with a pretty pink bow.
It's first place prize for winning who can run fastest
from God to the worldly boat.

I'm tired of stretching, yearning, yelling, to get out
with words that only land a slingshot
distance away.
We are a generation of people
that declared, "Prayers don't work, so do it yourself"
We are scared all the time and
it's rare if we know any inkling
of who we are, because that's
exactly the anxieties we bear
So if I may share, the answer of long
awaited prayers···

"For God so loved the world He gave
His one and only Son, so that everyone who
believes in Him will not perish but have
everlasting life."

Engulfed

Our generation doesn't have to be in strife.
To be buried alive with the sins of our fleshly lives.
We can die daily to the past self,
and live in Jesus' sacrifice.
Be engulfed in the love of Christ.
He died to give you life.

A Divine exchange that didn't cost you anything,
but cost Him everything because He paid that price!
Burned, beaten, and broken, tortured
Beyond what you would be able to recognize.
Our Christ, walked with the cross, blood accumulating in his
lungs.
Back splayed, spit in His face,
The Lamb Had no one.
Humiliated, isolated, freshly pounded nails had Him hung.

With gleaming thorns upon His brow, The Son of God gave a
shout.
"Eloi, Eloi lema sabachthani?
"My God, my God, why have you deserted me?"
I'm telling you this because the youth need to realize the value
Of the blood that was spilled.
Jesus died an innocent man!
For the sins we committed He was killed!
He took the bill, while we sit here all chill
Looking the part but live in unbelief.
Jesus rose out of the grave, death was put into defeat.
He took the keys, the devil had to flee, silenced the Pharisees, and
He walked out in victory.
You and I have to stop with the "faith appearanced" tweets
And humble ourselves to the one who sits on the mercy seat.

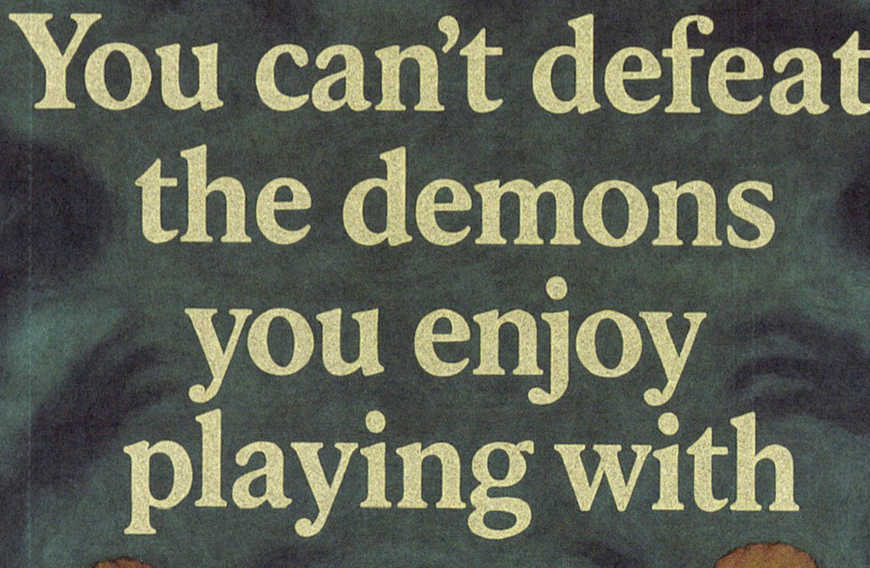

You can't defeat
the demons
you enjoy
playing with

THE PRAYER

Holy Spirit,

I give You permission to perform surgery. I have been playing with things that hurt me. I have been tiptoeing to the devil's beat, thinking I was strong enough to handle it. I was wrong.

Cut away the weeds. Pull out the thorns, even if it hurts. I am tired of my prayers feeling like rocks that fall to the ground. I want to be engulfed in Your love, not in my sin. Stitch me back together.

Amen.

SELAH

The poem speaks about "weeds" that aren't dandelions, but thorns. What is one habit or relationship you are holding onto that is actually pricking you?

Day 6

THE WAITING ROOM

THE ANCHOR

"Wait for the Lord; be strong and take heart and wait for the Lord."

— Psalm 27:14

THE POEM

The Waiting Room

I've been knocking on heaven's door
But it feels like nobody's home.
I'm sitting in the waiting room, feeling alone.
Checking the clock,
Checking my pulse,
Wondering if my prayers are just hitting the vault
Of the ceiling and bouncing back down to the floor.
Lord, I've been here before.

The silence is loud, it's deafening.
It's threatening to convince me that
You've left the building.
Maybe I'm too broken for healing.
But then I remember the seed.

When it's buried in the dirt, it looks like a grave.

It looks like the end, like it couldn't be saved.
But the darkness isn't a tomb, it's a womb.
You aren't ignoring me, You're growing me.
You're expanding my roots so I don't topple over
When the blessing finally blooms.

I wanted a microwave answer, quick and hot.
You're giving me a slow-cooked crockpot
Kind of character.
So I will wait.
Not because I understand the delay,
But because I trust the One who holds the day.
Silence isn't absence,
It's just the deep breath before the sentence
"It is finished."

THE PRAYER
God of the Wait,
The silence is hard. I feel forgotten. But I choose to believe that
You are working in the unseen. I trust that I am being planted, not
buried.
Give me the patience to endure this season. Develop my character
while I wait for my answer. I will not interpret Your silence as
absence. I will wait for the bloom.
Amen.

The
darkness
isn't a tomb,
it's a
womb.

SELAH

What is one prayer you have almost given up on? Write it down one more time here, and surrender the timeline to God.

I asked for a repair,
You gave me a demolition.
I asked for a bandage,
You gave me a physician.

PART II:
THE CONSTRUCTION
(The Encounter)

Day 7
RESCUE

THE ANCHOR

"In my distress I called to the Lord; I cried to my God for help. From his temple he heard my voice; my cry came before him, into his ears. He reached down from on high and took hold of me; he drew me out of deep waters."

— Psalm 18:6, 16

THE POEM

Rescue

The alarms struck in heaven, and I arrived to find
That torment entwined your mind and soul.
They bent and cracked your spine and turned your prayers fetal.

It's straight up evil.
I see the hurt shoved deep inside
How shallow the covered−up skin is riddled with scars
It tears my heart

I didn't want it to turn out this way
But my child, I'm here anyways.
Here to the beckoning call of desperate cries

Rescue

Of "God I'm done trying!"

You told me you were at your limit.
But where in your equation did you plug in the infinity
Of My majesty
So that it equaled victory?

But..
Over and over, I will race to save you.
There isn't a universe that exists
Where my hands won't assist
I love you/ Te amo/ Je t'aime/ ani ohev okta
Languages cannot express the depths that I will persist
The I AM is in the midst

I AM your strong tower
I AM your rest
I AM your strength when you have nothing else left
Child you are MINE!

My Pride, My joy, My creation divine
Nothing formed against you shall stand because
Your Father is here to stay
If you haven't already guessed
Because...
I hear you whisper underneath your breath,
I hear you whisper you have nothing left...

Where in your equation
did you plug in the
infinity of My majesty?

THE PRAYER

Father,

I have been looking at my problems through the lens of my own limitations. I looked at the math of my life—my resources, my strength, my past—and I calculated defeat. I forgot to add You to the equation.

Thank You that when my alarms ring, You do not hesitate. You race to save me. Thank You that You are fluent in my pain, speaking love in every language my heart needs to hear. I will stop trying to fix this on my own. I let You be the Tower. I let You be the Strength.

I am Yours.

Amen.

SELAH

Look at the biggest stressor in your life right now. How does the situation change if you factor in God's infinity? Write the new "equation" below.

Day 8
I FOUND IT
(THE MISSING PIECE)

THE ANCHOR

"She gave this name to the Lord who spoke to her: 'You are the God who sees me,' for she said, 'I have now seen the One who sees me.'"

— Genesis 16:13

THE POEM

I Found It

I finally found it!
The missing piece, the answer to why my soul exists.
So if you could permit
I'd like to emit this found treasure
So you too will have a heart convict.

My heart found its Savior beloved
He came in the form of a dove that came from above.
God wrapped in flesh, shoved into humanity
To rid the world of its sin calamity
Oh, I found Him!

El roi, the God who sees, who sought me even when
I didn't look in His direction.
He left an impression.
Praise is my soul's expression,
Its confession to the one whose mind, body, and spirit is His
possession.
Jesus is His name.

And I pray that you can proclaim
That your souls found its King
To the one that reigns supreme.

THE PRAYER
El Roi, The God Who Sees,
Thank You for finding me when I wasn't even looking for You.
Thank You for being the missing piece that makes the picture of my
life make sense. I am tired of the "calamity" of sin. I accept the peace
of Your presence.
You possess my mind, body, and spirit. Reign supreme in my life
today.
Amen.

El Roi, the God who sees.
Who sought me even when
I didn't look in His direction.

SELAH

Describe a moment in your life where you felt "seen" by God, even when you felt invisible to people.

____

____

____

____

____

____

____

____

____

____

____

____

____

____

____

____

____

____

____

____

____

____

____

____

Day 9

THE BREATH

THE ANCHOR

"The Spirit of God has made me; the breath of the Almighty gives me life."

— Job 33:4

THE POEM

The Breath

I used to think You were a ghost
A spooky vapor that I feared the most.
Something intangible, unreachable,
A force that was completely unteachable.

But then I realized, I was missing the mark.
You aren't a ghost in the dark.
You are the breath in my lungs.
The wind that fills the sails when the song is sung.

The Paraclete, the Advocate, the Comforter close.
The one who knows me the most.
When I don't have the words to pray,
You intercede with groans that words can't say.

You're the GPS when I'm lost in the woods.
The power to do what I never thought I could.
It's not by might, nor by power,
But by Your Spirit that I bloom like a flower.

So fill me up, Holy Spirit, overflow.
I want to go where You want me to go.
I'm tired of running on empty fumes.
Come and fill up all of these rooms.
Be the fire, be the wind, be the peace.
Let Your presence in me never cease.

THE PRAYER
Holy Spirit,
I invite You in. Fill the rooms of my heart that I have kept locked.
Breathe new life into my dry bones. I stop trying to live this Christian
life on my own power.
Be my GPS. Be my Advocate. When I don't know what to pray,
pray through me. I surrender to Your wind. Blow where You want to
blow.
Amen.

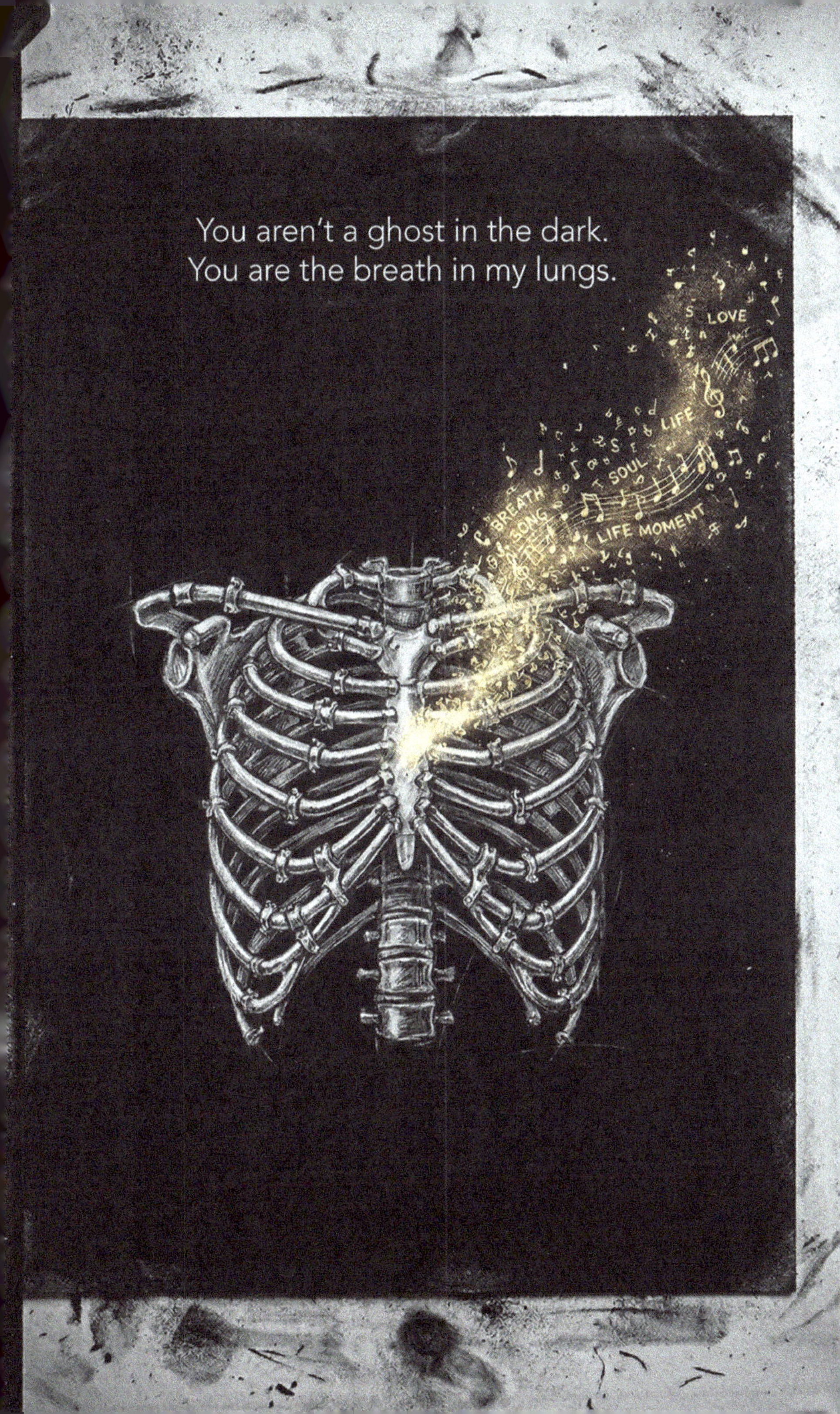

You aren't a ghost in the dark.
You are the breath in my lungs.
LOVE
LIFE
BREATH
SOUL
SONG
LIFE MOMENT

SELAH

The Holy Spirit is often called the "Comforter." In what area of your life do you need comfort right now? Ask Him to meet you there.

Day 10
RELEASING CONTROL

THE ANCHOR
"Trust in the Lord with all your heart and lean not on your own understanding; in all your ways submit to him, and he will make your paths straight."
— Proverbs 3:5-6

THE POEM

Releasing Control
It's time to let it go.
I've been holding on to the keys of control
Because my way seemed safer but it has led to my woe.
This feeling though, freedom filling my soul
It's whole.
For the first time in forever
The burden on my shoulders is disrobed
Your word teaches me that
I should trust you with all my heart and lean not on my understanding
That my path would be straight and ever expanding.
Your way for me is good and your plan for me
Is only for advancing, enhancing the mold

That the potter has deemed outstanding.
It's time to let go and be a living sacrifice
To the one that deserves to be magnified.
It's time to let it go.

THE PRAYER

Master Potter,

My hands are tired from gripping the wheel. I have tried to steer my own life because I was afraid of where You might take me. But my way has led to woe.

I hand You the keys. I trust Your mold. Do what You need to do to enhance me, advance me, and make me like Jesus. I am ready to be a living sacrifice.

Amen.

Your plan for me is only for
ADVANCING,
enhancing the mold that the potter has deemed outstanding.

SELAH

What is one specific area (finances, relationships, career) where you are still terrified to let go of the keys?

Day 11

RISE

THE ANCHOR

"Do not gloat over me, my enemy! Though I have fallen, I will rise. Though I sit in darkness, the Lord will be my light."
— Micah 7:8

THE POEM

Rise

In the stillness of the stars, I stand in the shadow,
Knotted in a net of notorious deeds,
A canvas of chaos, a life lived shallow,
Where will wavers and the war of want proceeds.

Mistakes mount, marking my mind's map,
Caught in a carousel of constant contrition,
Like Eve, the original offender, in sin's trap,
Grasping greedily, granting guilt's admission.

But then, a beacon breaks the blackness bold,
A carpenter's cry, a cross to cancel the cost,
His history, healing hands hold,
A narrative of nectar, for the needy and the lost.

So, I step, soaked in a stream of steadfast love,
A sinner, sure, but swathed in a sea of salvation,
For every falter, forgiveness fits like a glove,
And in His haven, my hiccups find their station.

I rise, renewed, from the ruins of remorse,
A voyager venturing on a voyage vast,
In the Creator's compass, I commit my course,
For every finale, a fresh future forecast.

THE PRAYER
Redeemer,
I have spent enough time in the ruins of remorse. I have let my
mistakes map my mind for too long. Today, I accept the "fresh future
forecast."
Thank You that Your forgiveness fits like a glove—tailor-made
for my mess. I commit my course to Your compass. I am standing up.
I am moving forward. The past is a lesson, not a life sentence.
Amen.

I rise, renewed,
from the ruins of
remorse.

SELAH

"For every finale, a fresh future forecast." What is one chapter of your life that has ended recently? What do you hope the new forecast looks like?

Day 12

THE MYSTERIOUS REALM OF THE SOUL

THE ANCHOR
"For we are God's handiwork, created in Christ Jesus to do good works, which God prepared in advance for us to do."
— Ephesians 2:10

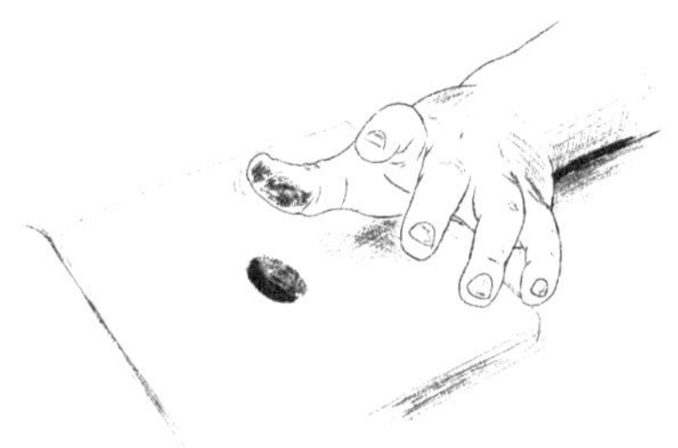

THE POEM

The Mysterious Realm of the Soul
Something happened today
That I didn't expect.
A memory risen while sharpening
a dull white and orange striped pencil.
How strange and fickle the human memory
Can be.

The most benign actions and details of life,
Triggering moments frozen in past.
It's the shaving and grinding of
Graphite, that i'm pulled by my nine year old self
Doing the same thing.

For reasons unbeknownst to me,

Creation Under Construction

I'm collecting the pulverized pencil
Dust and fingerprinting my classmates.
Each print collected, categorized, and recorded
In a booklet of my making.

All this, makes me wonder.
Although now larger, those smudges
Of nine year old's fingers, haven't changed.
The maps of patterns
Laid out on evermoving fingers.

Makes me think about
Another unchanging fingerprint,
The soul.
The essence of being a
Unique human.

An artisanal masterpiece of God,
that we still as of
Yet are still learning to comprehend.
This inner part,
Subconscious and unknown
The mysterious realm of the soul.

THE PRAYER
Artist of my Soul,
It is overwhelming to think that You designed the swirls on my
fingertips and the depth of my spirit. I am an artisanal masterpiece,
handcrafted by You.
When I feel small or ordinary, remind me of the mystery of my
own soul. Help me to honor the creation You have made in me. I
want to know You more, and in doing so, understand myself.
Amen.

An artisanal
masterpiece
of God.

SELAH

Take a moment to look at your own hand. Acknowledge that the God of the universe designed that specific pattern. Write a few sentences of praise for His attention to detail.

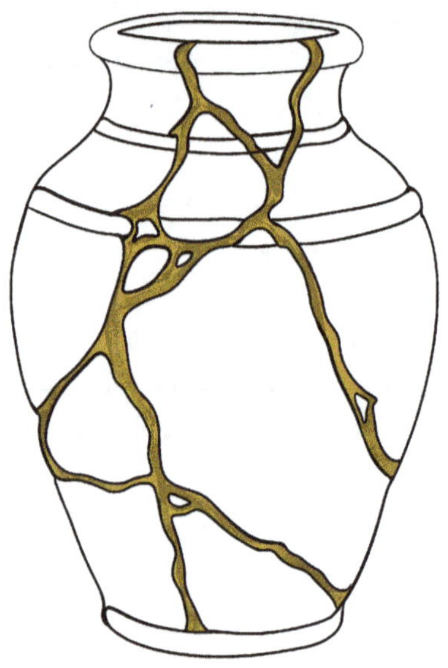

A silence that saves face
is a noise that costs a soul.
Open your mouth,
let the river flow.

PART III:
THE COMMISSION

Day 13

UNASHAMED

THE ANCHOR

"For I am not ashamed of the gospel, because it is the power of God that brings salvation to everyone who believes."

— Romans 1:16

THE POEM

Unashamed

Up to here, the Lord has helped me.
It wasn't until I looked back at my past
That I could clearly see.

What's kinda funny
Is how similar to a demolition site it looks.
All the lies, all the schemes,
All the sin I undertook.
Each one a charge of C4
Ready to explode my life to pieces
as any bomb should.

Enough Dynamite in one
Single punch, you would think it's

Unashamed

Floyd Mayweather's right hook.
But it's also like messed up pages, filled with tear stains
From eyes that ran out of fuel
And whiteout covered chapters I tried to
Erase out of my book.

It's not something I wanted anyone to read
That much I understood.
To be looked down, judged, labeled as something that's no good.

When I take the time to see it now
It changes from demolition to creation under construction.

A beautiful movie production, too great for an Oscar to cover.
Hollywood's imagination pales in comparison
To the purposes God has to
Make a total spiritual reversion.

So that's why I have so much conviction
From this process that I've been given
That I tell you this admission, that through Christ's crucifixion
You can break free from every circumstance and situation.

You're not too far, you're not worthless,
And you're not too dirty for God
Those are all lies from Satan.

Lord, you knew me before I was in my mother's womb
You knew all the things that I would do.
That's why I thank you now, because if you wouldn't have
Gracefully broken me, I'd had been stuck lying there doomed.
The pieces of my heart that had
More of me and less of You,
Now have the faith to say
To every mountain

Creation Under Construction

"Get up and move"

I'm grateful because you loved me enough
And stopped me from where I was headed to
Turned me back from the sin that
Had me so consumed.
My ears could no longer hear your voice
They were so untuned.

My eyes strained in the dark
In that path that I pursued,
I was so confused and bruised
And through all the hurt that people have construed⋯
I can imagine the devil was amused because
All the mess that ensued.
With up to my eyeballs in sin, I was subdued.

Everything was spinning around
just like Crash Bandicoot,
except every box I broke was filled with TNT
Ending the game with a big Kaboom.
I didn't think it through to tell you the truth.
But that didn't matter to you.

So much grace grew and bloomed and
Infused into this tattered soul you exhumed⋯
Jesus you had compassion, just like with Lazarus
When you raised him from his tomb.
In all this I tell you... I am unashamed.
Because He said to me, "My grace is sufficient for you,
For power is perfected in weakness"
Therefore I will most gladly boast all the more
About my weaknesses, so that Christ's
Power may reside in me.

Unashamed

So because of Christ, I am pleased
In weakness, in insults, in catastrophes.
In persecutions and in pressures.
For when I am weak, then I am strong.

I am unashamed
Because I am no longer a slave to sin
But a child of God.
His blood flows through these veins.
He baptized me in living waters
And I am forever changed.
So I invite you to make this same claim.
To let go of your life in the world
And all of its shame.

There's only one name above all names, the one who breaks
every chain
And that name is Jesus
The one who will forever reign,
The one who's glory cannot be contained,
The one who's every knee will bow and every tongue will confess
That He alone will rule this domain.

I am unashamed.
Stone of my help,
There was no one else.
You picked me up,
For when what I sowed, was dealt.
Jesus you took my burden upon yourself and
Nailed it on the cross to be repelled.
Every lash, every sin and sickness could be felt.
You did it all without one protest to be expelled,
Such love for me you upheld⋯.
Just so that the accusations from the enemy could be dispelled,

My friends be unashamed, there's no time left to dwell
Rain or shine, take the hand of Christ
I promise through it all, it is well.

THE PRAYER

God of My Story,

I stop hiding my past. I stop trying to "whiteout" the chapters I am ashamed of. I realize now that the demolition was necessary for the construction.

Use my story. Use the messed-up pages. Let my life be a testimony that no one is too far, too dirty, or too worthless for Your grace. I am not a slave to sin; I am a child of God. I am unashamed.

Amen.

It changes from demolition
to creation under construction.

SELAH

Who is one person in your life who needs to hear your story? Not the polished version, but the "creation under construction" version?

Day 14

FORGIVENESS

THE ANCHOR

"Be kind and compassionate to one another, forgiving each other, just as in Christ God forgave you."

— Ephesians 4:32

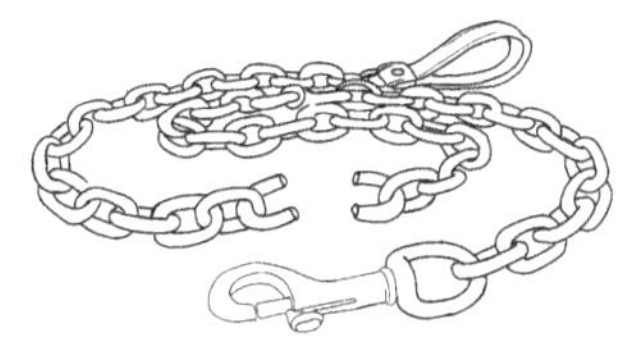

THE POEM

Forgiveness

Forgiveness feels like a fragile flower, flourishing in the face of fierce foes

Nowadays it just feels more fragile than it does fierce.

Easily is it bruised by the thorn of memories past

Pain that was poured out as wrath

Poking holes of flashbacks on neuron paths.

Jesus said that we ought to forgive seventy times seven mistakes

After offense 491, I grab at the excuse to execute every

Silent treatment tactic and enforce evasive maneuvers

That no apology can rectify.

The misdeeds and errors testify against their worthiness

Of my forgiveness.

Creation Under Construction

Like mending shattered glass, the pieces may join,
But the fault lines remain, a testament to the breaking.

Memories' marred mosaic with platitudes plastering the pieces
precariously.
I hold on to my hurt happily⋯.am I?
This grudge that I hold on to looks like
Vengeance wrapped in self-righteous piety
To justify my need to hold onto my bitterness.
I've had it walking with me on a tightly held leash
Giving it treats and grooming it as if my victimhood
Was on display at a show.

"But if you do not forgive others of their sins, your Father will
not forgive yours"
Don't you know how much they hurt me God?
With no regard to how it would affect me?
Then they just say sorry again and again, the cycle never ends
And you're asking me to just accept that?

Grace . Still and quiet.
Grace . A word that takes down the unforgiveness giant.
Grace . It disarms my iron clad argument.

My grace is sufficient for you.
When I said that I didn't mean, just⋯you.
If 491 was the limit of forgiveness
Your number has surpassed the threshold
But child of mine I don't even keep count.
Your trespass landed in the abyss as soon as
Your humility brought your knees to the ground.

I know it hurts.
It hurts me too.

I do not stand idly by
As much as you believe that to be true.
They're my child too.

A Father corrects those He loves and
I very much love all of you
Equally, unequivocally.

I will deal with the offense
In my judgement, in my justice.
So, forgive my daughter.
Forgive, my son.
Forgive as I have forgiven you
Not because they deserve it
But because your obedience is
Greater than your vengeance.
Embrace empathy, elevate existence, and experience the essence
of eternal forgiveness.

THE PRAYER
Father,
This is hard. I want justice, but You are asking for mercy. I have
been walking my bitterness on a leash, treating it like a pet, when I
should have cast it out.
Help me to drop the leash. I choose to forgive [Name(s)] today.
Not because what they did was right, but because You have forgiven
me a thousand times over. I trust You to handle the justice. I choose
the freedom of grace.
Amen.

Your obedience is greater
than your vengeance.

Is there a "giant" of unforgiveness you are facing? Write down the name of the person you need to forgive, and then physically cross it out as a sign of release.

Day 15

STRETCHER BEARERS

THE ANCHOR
"Carry each other's burdens, and in this way you will fulfill the law of Christ."
— Galatians 6:2

THE POEM

Stretcher Bearers
They say it takes a village to raise a child
But what does it take to save a soul running wild?
It takes a few crazy friends.

The kind who don't care about the trends.
The kind who will rip the roof off the place
Just to get you face to face with Grace.

I'm talking about the ones who carry your mat
When you're paralyzed by fear and can't do this or that.
When your faith is too weak to walk on its own,
They pick you up so you're not alone.

We weren't meant to be islands in the sea.

We were meant to be branches on the same tree.
So find your stretcher bearers, the ones who will fight.
Who will pray you through the darkest night.

And when you're strong, return the favor.
Be the hands and feet of the Savior.
Carry the burden, lift up the weak.
Speak life to the ones who can't even speak.
Because we are the body, not just a collection of parts.
Connected by the beating of Jesus' heart.

THE PRAYER

Lord,

I confess I have tried to walk this road alone. I have been too proud to ask for help, or too afraid to let people see my paralysis.

Thank You for the stretcher bearers in my life. Thank You for the community that carries me when I cannot walk. Help me to be that friend for someone else. Show me who needs their burden lifted today.

Amen.

WE WEREN'T MEANT TO BE ISLANDS IN THE SEA.
WE WERE MEANT TO BE BRANCHES ON THE SAME TREE.

SELAH

Take a moment to truly pause and reflect on the concept of your "stretcher bearers." This phrase, rooted in the biblical account of the paralytic man whose friends carried him to Jesus, represents the vital people in your life who bear your burdens, sustain you in your weakness, and faithfully bring you into the presence of healing, hope, and strength. They are the friends, family members, mentors, or colleagues who don't just offer sympathy but actively engage in the heavy lifting required during your most challenging times.

Who are these selfless individuals who have carried you—whether literally or figuratively—through a period of illness, grief, professional setback, or profound personal struggle? Their effort is often unseen, and their fidelity is priceless.

Do not let their dedication go unacknowledged. **Send a text to one of your stretcher bearers right now and thank them for carrying you.** Be specific about the time or situation where their support made a difference, allowing your gratitude to be a specific affirmation of their faithful love. Acknowledging their effort is a powerful act of relational stewardship. **Think of a specific person and a specific moment when they were your "stretcher bearer," and briefly describe that moment and why their action meant so much to you.**

Day 16

NIGHT SHIFT

THE ANCHOR
"Put on the full armor of God, so that you can take your stand against the devil's schemes."
— Ephesians 6:11

THE POEM
Night Shift
The sun goes down and the gloves come off.
It's the night shift, where the demons don't scoff,
They attack.
Intrusive thoughts dressed in all black
Sneaking through the cracks of my fatigue.

It's a major league battle for my peace of mind.
"You're a failure," "You're unlovable," "You're running out of time."
Arrows flying at my head like I'm standing on the front line
Without a helmet.

I feel hell-bent on destruction,
My anxiety functioning at full production.

But wait.

I forgot who I am.
I forgot that I don't fight for victory, I fight from victory.
I'm reaching for the armory.

Ephesians 6, I'm suiting up.
Helmet of Salvation, check.
Breastplate of Righteousness, protecting the neck.
Shield of Faith to quench every fiery dart,
Whether it's panic, depression, or a broken heart.
I pull out the Sword of the Spirit, which is the Word.
And I swing it at the lies that I've heard.

"Get behind me, Satan!"
I'm not a victim in the dark, I'm a child of the Light.
The blood of Jesus is the power that helps me fight.
So try if you want, bring your best shot.
But I'm standing on the Rock that cannot be bought,
Cannot be moved, cannot be shaken.
The devil thought he had me, but he was mistaken.

THE PRAYER

Commander of Angel Armies,

When the night comes and the thoughts attack, remind me that I am not defenseless. I put on Your armor now. I cover my mind with Salvation. I guard my heart with Your Righteousness.

I rebuke the lies that say I am a failure. I speak Your Word over my anxiety. I am not a victim. I am a victor. The darkness cannot stay when the Light steps in.

Amen.

I don't fight for victory,
I fight from victory.

SELAH

What is the most common "fiery dart" (lie) the enemy throws at you at night? Find one Bible verse that contradicts it and write it here.

Day 17

STAINED GLASS

THE ANCHOR

"On hearing this, Jesus said to them, 'It is not the healthy who need a doctor, but the sick. I have not come to call the righteous, but sinners.'"

— Mark 2:17

THE POEM

Stained Glass

I walked into the building looking for a hospital
But I found a museum.
Statues of "perfect" people, or at least that's how I see 'em.
I showed them my scars and they handed me a mask.
"Cover that up," they said, "That's too much to ask."
"We don't do messy here, we only do blessed."

So I left, feeling distressed, depressed, and unimpressed.
Thinking if this is God, I don't want it.
If this is love, you can keep the bonnet
And the Sunday best.

I was ready to throw the baby out with the bathwater,

Ready to run like a prodigal daughter.
But then Jesus met me in the parking lot.
He said, "They didn't die for you. I did."

He said, "Don't confuse the fan club with the Player."
Don't confuse the building with the Savior.
People are broken glass, sharp and jagged.
They cut you because they're ragged.
But Jesus is the glazier.

He's the one who takes the shards and makes a mosaic.
He didn't come for the healthy, He came for the sick.
He flipped tables on the hypocrites, and that's the trick.
He hates the mask more than I do.

So I won't let a Pharisee keep me from the Mercy Seat.
I won't let "church folk" keep me from touching His feet.
I'm following Christ, not the crowd.
And if that makes me an outcast,
Then I'll sing His praises loud.
Unashamed.

THE PRAYER

Jesus,

I have been hurt by Your people. I have been cut by the broken glass of the church. But I know that You are the Healer, not the hurter.

Help me to forgive the "museum" and seek the Hospital. I will not let the hypocrisy of others keep me from the Mercy Seat. You are the Glazier, and You are making something beautiful out of this mess. I choose You.

Amen.

DON'T CONFUSE
THE FAN CLUB
with the Player.

SELAH

Have you ever walked away from God because of something a person said or did? It's easy to let the mistakes or actions of others cloud your view of faith. Tell God right now that you are separating His perfect character, which is unchanging, from their fallible human actions.

Day 18

SELLOUT CHRISTIANS

THE ANCHOR

"Do not conform to the pattern of this world, but be transformed by the renewing of your mind."

— Romans 12:2

THE POEM

Sellout Christians

There's something that I've come to share today.
Something that has been put on public display
And brought decay to the reputation of the Church and
Put into disarray.
There has been a "trend" that church has to look like the world
And be "contemporary"
It has been made to look like
Holiness is unnecessary
As if it were a mere suggestion of a word instead
Of it being mandatory.
But being Holy wasn't a suggestion by God.
It's an action verb, a state of being, a commandment
From the Most High
Adonai

Invite the Holy Spirit to occupy
Seperate from wrong to do
What's right
Don't be a sellout Christian
In order to appear attractive to the world
When we're made to look like Christ.

THE PRAYER

Holy God, Adonai,

I confess that I sometimes want to fit in. I downplay my faith to be "relevant" or "cool." But You did not call me to blend in; You called me to be set apart.

Renew my mind. Teach me that holiness is not a burden, but a beauty. I want to look like Christ, even if it looks strange to the world. I will not sell out.

Amen.

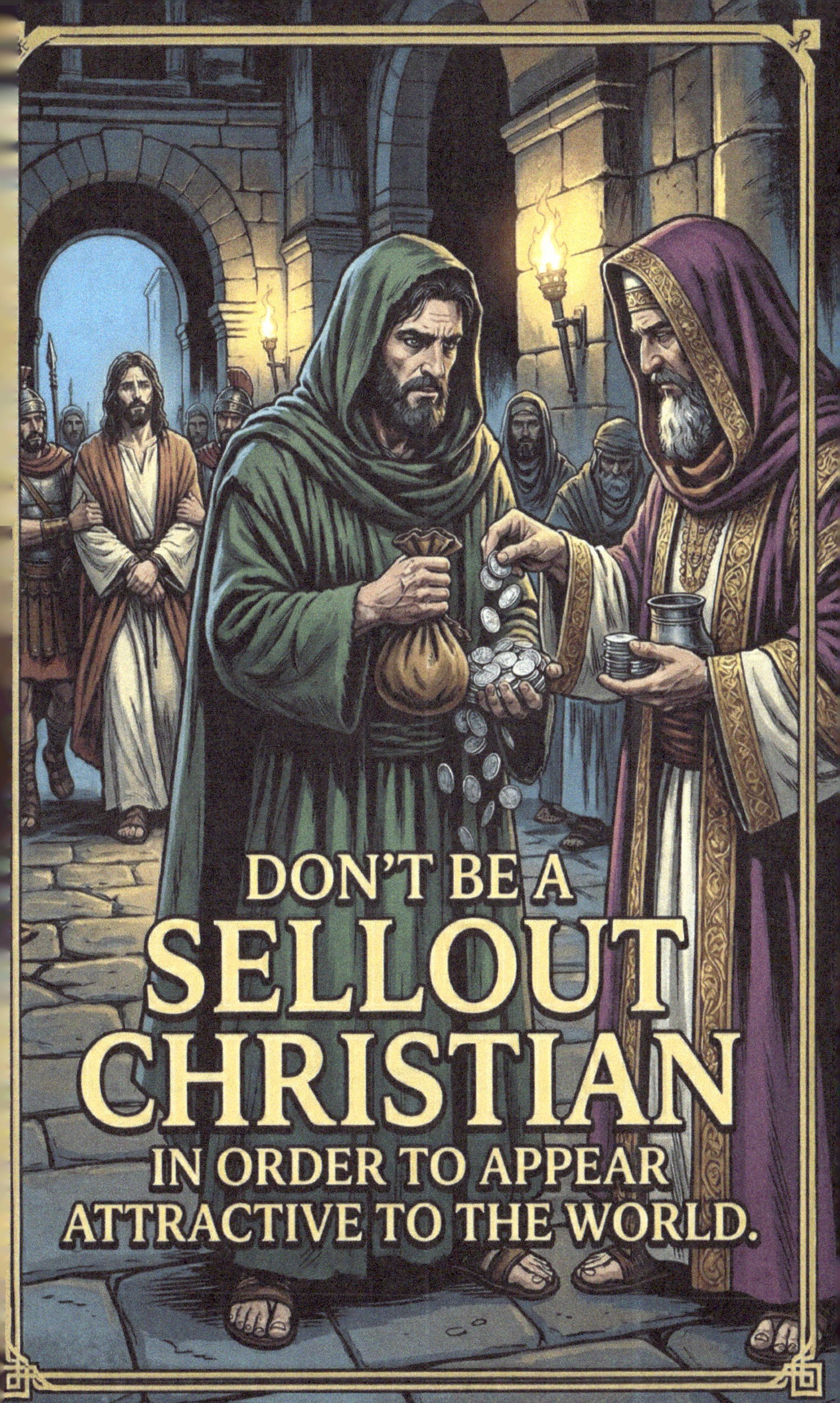

DON'T BE A
SELLOUT
CHRISTIAN
IN ORDER TO APPEAR
ATTRACTIVE TO THE WORLD.

SELAH

In what area of your life (speech, entertainment, relationships) have you compromised to "fit in"?

Day 19

MIDNIGHT MELODY

THE ANCHOR

"About midnight Paul and Silas were praying and singing hymns to God, and the other prisoners were listening to them."
— Acts 16:25

THE POEM

Midnight Melody

The chains are heavy and the cell is dark.
The situation is bleak and stark.
My back is bleeding and my heart is sore.
I don't think I can take anymore.

But then I remember Paul and Silas.
In the middle of the mess, they didn't stay silent.
They started to sing.
A melody to the King.

It didn't make sense to the natural eye.
To praise God when you're ready to die.
But that's the secret, that's the key.
Worship is the weapon that sets us free.

It shakes the foundations, it breaks the locks.
It turns the prison into a paradox.
So I'm tuning my heart to the sound of heaven.
Counting my blessings, reaching eleven.

I will sing in the shadow, I will shout in the rain.
I will praise Your name through the grief and the pain.
Because You are worthy, no matter the circumstance.
So I'm choosing to sing, I'm choosing to dance.

Let the walls fall down, let the chains break loose.
I'm cutting the enemy's noose.
With a midnight melody, a song of the free.
God, I worship You, for You are with me.

THE PRAYER

God of the Midnight Hour,

It is dark, and I am tired. But I choose to open my mouth and sing. I choose to weaponize my worship against the despair.

You are worthy when the sun is shining, and You are worthy when the cell is dark. Let my praise shake the foundations of my anxiety. Break the chains of fear. I am singing my way out.

Amen.

It turns the prison
into a paradox.
Worship is the
weapon that
sets us free.

SELAH

Put on your favorite worship song right now. Sing it loud, even if you don't feel like it. Write down how your mood changes after the song ends.

Day 20
INTERRUPTING ETERNITIES

THE ANCHOR
"Therefore go and make disciples of all nations, baptizing them in the name of the Father and of the Son and of the Holy Spirit."
— Matthew 28:19

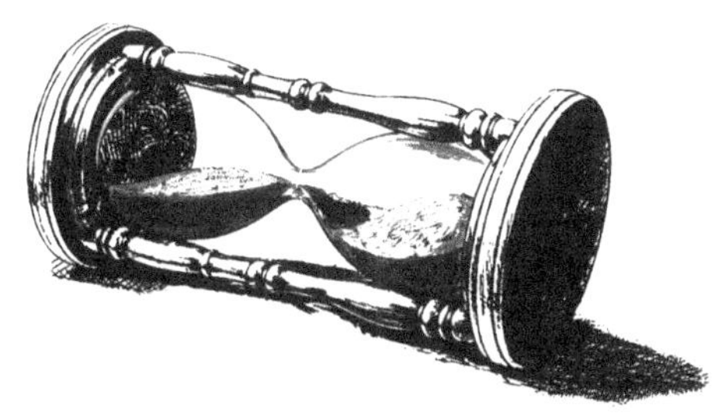

THE POEM
Interrupting Eternities
"Simon, son of Jonah, do you love me?"
"Tend my sheep."
How many neglected sheep
Are out there,
Ones that haven't heard
The news of a Savior?

In my needless comforting life,
How many chances have I
Let slip by to tell someone
About Jesus?
When did I stop extending
the hands of Christ
And instead, go through the motions

Creation Under Construction

Of mediocre Christianity?

I am convicted of my inaction.
My lack of boldness for the
Gospel.
We were called to be
Nation Preachers,
Kingdom seekers.
Broken heart reachers.

Our mission is to
Interrupt the eternities
Of those who live by
The world.
Those destined for fire
And separation from God.
That is the cost of a life without a Savior.

No time can be lost not
Delivering the good news!
An anguish for the lost
Must fill you.

Your unsaved family,
Friends, neighbors, coworkers,
Strangers.
The cost will be forever!
"Do you love me?"
"Tend my sheep."
Interrupt Eternities.

OUR MISSION IS TO
INTERRUPT
THE
ETERNITIES.

THE PRAYER

Lord of the Harvest,

Forgive my inaction. I have been comfortable while eternity is at stake. Break my heart for what breaks Yours. Give me the boldness to speak up, to reach out, to interrupt the path of destruction with the Good News.

I love You, Lord. Help me to tend Your sheep. Use me today to change someone's forever.

Amen.

SELAH

Write down the name of one person who does not know Jesus. Pray for an opportunity to "interrupt their eternity" this week.

Creation Under Construction

Father,

As I close this book, I realize that the construction is not over. The scaffolding of progress is still up. The renovation continues. I look around at the unfinished corners of my heart and the areas where the drywall is still dusty, and for the first time, I don't feel the need to hide the mess. There's no shame in being molded into Your Masterpiece.

I am no longer afraid of the process. I am no longer terrified of the demolition because I know that You do not tear down to destroy; You tear down to rebuild something eternal. I am finished with the exhaustion of trying to present a "finished product" to You. I finally understand that I don't have to wait until the dust settles or the cracks are filled to come into Your presence. You aren't looking for a polished showroom; You are looking for a willing spirit.

Lord, I lay down the heavy burden of old "church hurt"—the times I was told I was too broken to be useful or that my mess made me unwelcome in Your house. I release the weight of those who pointed at the scaffolding and called it a failure. I choose to trust Your blueprint over their opinions. I am no longer held back by the fear of being "unfit," because You are the one who declared this site holy.

I know that You are the Architect, and Your plans are good—far better than the plans I tried to draft for myself. I am not a mistake. I am not a condemned building. I am Your temple, Your masterpiece, fearfully and wonderfully made, even in the midst of this ongoing renovation. Thank You for seeing the finished home even when I can only see the rubble.

Keep building me. Keep breaking me if You must, for I know Your hands are gentle even when they are firm. Strip away the "default" layers of my old self and replace them with the infusion of Your Spirit. Don't let me settle for a quick fix or a superficial coat of paint. Just don't stop until the work is complete. Don't stop until I look like Jesus.

I submit my site to You. I leave the tools in Your hands.

I love You.

In Jesus' name,

Amen.

Acknowledgements

This project, much like the life it describes, was not built in isolation. It took a team of kind souls, a patient Creator, and a community of believers to move these words from a quiet dream into the book you hold in your hands.

To my Family: You have been the steady pillars of my life. To my parents, you have raised me in the path of The Lord and formed me into the woman that I am today. Mom, you are the force behind me turning my poetry into a book. Without you, this wouldn't have been possible. Thank you for witnessing my hardest moments and my best ones, and for loving me through every single stage of my growth. You've seen me when I was struggling to find the right words and when I was overwhelmed by the weight of my own story. You are my home, and I am so deeply grateful for the warmth and safety you have always provided for me.

To my Church, Iglesia Génesis: Thank you for being a place where it is safe to grow. Without you, this book would not be here today. You have been a sanctuary for my spirit and a constant reminder that God is always working in our lives, even when we can't see the progress. Thank you for being a community that values the journey as much as the destination. Vamos Por Más!

To Monica, my Editor: Thank you for seeing the heart within my messy first drafts. You didn't just look at these poems as text on a page; you cared for the vision behind them. Your keen eye and gentle guidance helped refine these words without losing their raw honesty. Thank you for walking beside me through the long hours of perfecting this story and for believing in its message as much as I do.

To Kailee, my Illustrator: Thank you for bringing the soul of this book to life. You took the abstract feelings of my heart—the light, the shadows, and the hope—and turned them into a stunning reality. Your art made the invisible parts of my journey visible, and I am in awe of how you captured the spirit of these words so perfectly.

To my Discord Community: You have been the greatest support system I could ever ask for. Thank you for the endless encouragement, the kindness of a listening ear, and for being a community that truly understands the beauty of sharing our stories. Your presence kept me going when the task felt too big, and your support gave me the courage to be vulnerable.

Above all, to my Heavenly Father: Thank you for never giving up on me. Thank you for Your relentless grace and for the love that continues to transform my soul every single day. I am humbled that You would use my life and my words to reflect Your light.

Vivian Figueroa

Acknowledgements

About the Author

Vivian Figueroa is a dynamic poet, compelling spoken word artist, and an unwavering believer who openly acknowledges that she is a work perpetually "under construction." Her creative endeavors delve deep into the human experience, utilizing the powerful tools of rhythm and rhyme to explore the often-gritty, unvarnished reality of maintaining faith in a complex world.

Her artistry serves as a candid exploration of profound themes, including the challenging and necessary journey of addressing mental health, the constant struggle for spiritual clarity, and, most centrally, the relentless, unconditional grace of God. She does not shy away from the difficult parts of her testimony, finding beauty and truth in imperfection.

This collection of work—a raw and honest compilation of her poetry and spoken word—is more than just art; it is her living testimony. Through it, Vivian aims to provide a powerful message of hope and redemption, declaring with conviction that no soul is ever too broken, too far gone, or too damaged to receive God's love and undergo a complete spiritual renovation. Her voice is a beacon for those who are struggling, proving that transformation is always possible, even when the construction process is ongoing.

Connect with Vivian:

Instagram: @vivthepoet
TikTok: @vivthepoet
Website: www.vivianfigueroa.com

A Small Ask, A Big Impact

God uses ordinary things to reach extraordinary people.
Maybe He used this devotional for you. If so, I'd love your
help getting it into the hands of others who are ready to stop
hiding, start healing, and building with Jesus.

Leaving a review on Amazon is one of the simplest ways you
can extend that reach. As a self-published, first-time author, I
don't have a big publishing house behind me — just faith, a
story to tell, and readers like you.

If something in these pages resonated, challenged, or
encouraged you, please take a moment to share it on Amazon.
Your testimony could be the nudge someone else needs to
finally pick this up and they are precious gifts for me as well.

Thank you!
Vivian